The Fine Trousers of Almidano Artifoni and other poems

A rhyming romp through Joyce's Wandering Rocks

RUSSELL RAPHAEL

For Claire, who has no intention of reading Ulysses

The Fine Trousers of Almidano Artifoni and other poems

CONTENTS

PREFACE

Oh no! Not another guide to Ulysses! Well I hope this is a little different in that it's short enough to be of no trouble, no trouble at all, taking as it does, the form of nineteen petite poems. Well, poems is to flatter, sort of bits of rhyme and fiddlyblibs. Joyce liked a made up word; he enjoyed taking liberties with language generally, for example he writes music with words in chapter 11 Sirens, and turns it inside out and upside down in chapter 14, Oxen of the Sun. And let's not go near Finnegans Wake!

Wandering Rocks. It's as different to the rest of Ulysses as are most chapters. Yet whereas one does well to even notice where some chapters begin and end, Wandering Rocks looks and feels different. It is nineteen very short stories, each demarked by a few dots, an elongated rhombus or some other flourish. These are like life-buoys, so navigation is easy! Or so one might think. The hull-holing rocks are deceptive and seem to wander until too late – bash!

So I try in this little book to help and by mode of 'poetry', hope to keep things light and fresh. Much of the poetry is frivolous, a little bawdy and disreputable; so it should fit right in.

Wandering Rocks, the tenth of eighteen chapters in James Joyce's Ulysses, sits, like the others anonymously. It was only Joyce's post-publication 'schemata', in particular the second addressed to Stuart Gilbert, that suggested that this

collection of vignettes might be called Wandering Rocks.
So named, after the treacherous waters somewhere around
the Bosphorus and notable for the advice given to
Odysseus to avoid at all costs if he hoped to make it back
to Ithaca. Not so readers of Ulysses who must negotiate
this choppy chapter. The stories by and large do not
conclude; they lure in just enough to leave us wanting
before if we are not careful, we are shoved hull first into a
rock or just as bad, becalmed and left high and dry. Ulysses
as a whole is an examination of human nature through the
prism of Dublin and thereby Joyce's relationship with the
city of his birth and its people. Arguably nowhere is this
brought into sharper focus than in this central chapter
Wandering Rocks.

In the schemata Joyce suggests certain stylistic triggers
peculiar to each chapter; the name, setting, time of day,
colour, style and even, for goodness sake, a bodily organ.
So for 'the Rocks' what do we have?

Place: the streets of Dublin
Time: around 3.15 in the afternoon.
Colour: none.
Art: Mechanics
Technic: Labyrinth
Organ: Blood.

What becomes readily apparent is that unlike other
chapters in which events proceed chronologically, here we
have a bird's eye view of the whole city and observe this
panorama documentary-style, by way of nineteen separate
events occurring broadly at once. From such cartographer

perspective Dublin's streets might sprawl like veins and arteries, conveying a body's life blood, the people, without which any city is a mere husk. It would probably also appear a complicated mess, something of a labyrinth.

That Joyce invites us to consider in this very chapter, the ancient labyrinth of Crete, created by Daedalus, must surely stir the brain cells. That Daedalus invented the wings for example, designed so he and his son Icarus could escape the labyrinth and their captor, the Minotaur. It would have worked too, had Icarus not flown too close to the sun. This was so significant to Joyce that he penned certain correspondence under the pseudonym 'S. Dedalus' and created Stephen Dedalus as a central and autobiographical protagonist. Why? One assumes this is entwined with Stephen's artistic manifesto promulgated in A Portrait of the Artist as a Young Man and alludes to the breaking free of the culturally binding nets of Ireland.

What also marks this chapter apart is that it is concerned, more than your average chapter, with stuff. Physical stuff. It is not immune from interior monologue but it plays out less in the head and more on the street. We walk these streets, feeling and touching. Bloom has been pounding them all day and will for some hours yet. If in this chapter we wear out some of our own shoe leather, we might wonder what is the point of his journey? Just where is he going? And what is the beginning middle and end of his wanderings?

For that matter, in what direction does ambition lie for this book? How close to the sun does it seek to strive? Not in any serious poetical direction that's for sure. The author (I have for purposes of grandeur, assumed the third person), has no poetic or creative writing antecedence and claims neither that or any other sort of 'cedence'. Nor can he claim a PhD in Joycism or the like. But in recent years he and Ulysses have gotten to know each other quite well and seem to enjoy each other's company. Flann O'Brien might have observed a small but unknown atomic transference bicycle-like, from book to author. More brazen exponents of Oxen of the Sun may say that it and he had become as fast friends as an arse and a shirt.

In consequence, the author has some views on the stories of Wandering Rocks which via this modest book, one poem per vignette, he'd like to convey. He hopes it might help. He does not claim for it any definitive status; his observations may well be wide of the mark but as James Joyce is not here to cast doubt we'll never know. We certainly aren't going to obey any professorial orthodoxy. That then is the ambition of the book. That some of it happens to rhyme simply reflects the author's mood at the time of writing, which he though pretty neat.

East Finchley 2023

1 THE VERY REVEREND

From Francis Xavier to road of Malahide
John Conmee SJ makes his cheery way.
He won't have glum, for he cannot abide
Ungrateful souls on this glorious day.

A one-legged beggar in sailor suit
Serenades the benign priest.
But no song nor sniv'lin' salute
Will procure the lucre he seeks.

Tram passengers all, Father Conmee observes.
A mansplained wife yawns into her glove.
That awkward chap, shaken and stirred
Would rather not meet his priest on the bus.

Father Conmee regrets the poor souls unsaved;
Millions 'cross Africa and Or'ent.
Ah well, if they choose to remain depraved
To the Devil they must be sent.

In Ireland fortunately no such errata
The church (RC of course) understands its role.
To support the God given societal strata;
Erin's aristocracy being the status quo.

But how to comprehend human disaster?
That boat sunk and hundreds lost.
Well, provided Hail Mary's were timely uttered,
We can gloss over corporeal cost.

So generally all's well in a world
Where sin is absolved once a week.
So, what, we should bow and applaud?
While ignoring the poor and the meek?

Well-meaning though he may be,
On his help the poor shouldn't count.
No one's suggesting simony
But what of sermons on mounts?

In Father Conmee's halcyon world
Perpetual upon St. Peter's Rock
The poor are fed by accepting the Word
And nourished within the obedient flock.

You may think me terribly unkind.
After all, he's to Artane on charity mission.
But does he arrive? Well I can't find,
Leastways not in my edition.

2   IS HE OR ISN'T HE?

The Castle was sniffing around
For Fenian secrets that mattered
Keeping its nose close to the ground
In a city politically fractured.

Of police informers Bloom had suspicions
There's rumour but he's not saying who.
Though tooraloom, tooraloom emissions
Might be an inkling of a clue.

3 THIRTY-TWO FEET PER SECOND

The speed of a thing that falls
Is a theorem quite hard to recall
Bloom gives it a try
We wondered why
And what is the point of it all?

With Genesis it's right to begin
And that fall into original sin.
Referenced in our book
By the time that it took
A thing to be a lower down thing.

Per second its thirty-two feet
And each second the whole thing repeats
So sense a fall or 'thirty-two'
And it's a bit of a clue
To some fraud or other deceit.

You'll know Corny of recent purview
And the hay blade on which he did chew
Well, when he spat out its juice,
The projectile took course
In an arc rather than plummeting true.

Contrast said flight with Molly's donation
For one legged beggar amelioration
No messing this time,
It bolts in straight line
Albeit missing its destination.

If her sin you're troubling to find
When surely Molly is just being kind,
Raise your eyes from the floor
To Blazes' visit at four
It's adultery Joyce has in mind.

You see, Jimbo's an utter neurotic
Imagining Nora lovers, prolific.
And adultery for Jim
Trumps police informing
So this vignette may be somewhat symbolic.

4 BOODY

Boody wasn't being rudy
Rather simply saying it plain.
Katey wasn't being matey
But stifling hunger pang

Maggy had to be the mummy
Moving saucepans on the range
And Dilly just naively silly
Expecting Pa might spare some change.

For as we'll see in number eleven
If you'd care to wait a little bit
Our Father who art not in heaven
Is something of a tit.

5   THE MAN THAT MADE THE PEACHES BLUSH

We've heard quite a lot about him
We've gotten quite excited
Don't expect much St. Augustine
Once Blazes gets ignited.

'Course one shouldn't rush to judge
Give the benefit of the doubt
Premature conclusions hard to budge
Let the truth and nothing but seep out.

Alas vignette five presents a faltering start.
Silky smooth tone and playboy air
Are unhelpful notches on the character chart;
Peaches blush aside fat pear.

Strutting in brogues, fruit-a-squeezing,
Staring down her blouse and bloomin' 'eck.
Her embonpoint may not be heaving
But did he really need to check?

Booze and small jar added to wicker basket.
Without latter no gift complete
And I'll bet half my weekly wage packet
It's Plumtree's Potted Meat.

More aphrodis'yac than groc'ry gift
From a scoundrel that's quite rotten
All designed to loosen Molly's shift
So his meat can go-a-pottin'.

Presumes to pinch flower from phallic vase
Yet the damning evidence is yet to come.
Patience! For that we must take a pause.
On hold for a phone call with Miss Dunne.

6 THE FINE TROUSERS OF ALMIDANO
ARTIFONI

I want to be like Almidano
He parlees the Italiano.
Once taught music to Senore Dedalus,
Now promenades in sturdy trousers.

I'd like to turn on for a while
That Latin Artifoni style,
For I so admire that man
Trotting for the Dalkey tram.

But even this worthy Ital'yan
Cannot shift Stephen from his plan.
Though like Bloom later, he has a go
And Dedalus placates: 'Ci rifletterò'.

Within stone's throw of Henry Gratt-on
He rolls his papers into a baton.
But unlike Bloom's earlier phallic symbol
His is for the tram to signal.

Reverting to those trousers Artifoni
Here called stout, there hint sturdy
Splitting hairs? Maybe, but pray, let it go
And rejoice in the kecks Almidano!

Sorry to report, his gesticulation
Fails to delay tram acceleration.
It's Dalkey bound but just too soon
For our Roman hero that afternoon.

Intrepid man, he'll still head t'ward Dalkey
Even if he has to walkee.
Perché you'll always be in with a shout
When trousers are solid as well as stout.

In short, Artifoni can't be beat
The chap we most want to meet.
Though incomplete must be his story
At least there's the trousers in all their glory.

I want to be like Almidano
Who parlees the Italiano
He's things to do, places to be:
'Scusi eh? Tante belle cose!'

7   WE'VE GOT YOUR NUMBER

That clever lady Miss Dunne
She really might be the one
Illuminator. Perhaps above all the others.
It was while she sat there alone,
Simply answering the phone,
That she revealed to us, the cad's true colours.

If one takes as the measure of a man
To be the deeds by which he stands
This here Blazes don't make for a hill o' beans.
'Twixt Liv'pool and Belfast don't quibble
For machinations manifest to visible
As you figure out just what that phone call means.

One pound seven and sixpence
Is the remunerative distance
One must shlep to buy all the bloomin' tickets.
The cost for a single bill-et?
Well, we really couldn't say.
But synapses are firing, so hang on just a minute.

See these tickets, they all go to Ulster.
But only two lucky stubs pass muster
For onward sojourn to L'pool 'cross the Irish Sea
Where, hopes the fiery impresario
To perform as Molly's lothario
In den of lust, well beyond the cuckold's reach.

But to part with ready money
Until he's certain of his honey
Is a risk this gambler considers unreli-ible.
So she's not to call and book 'till later
Presuming odds shorten in his favour
Once squeaky bed quoits do the jaunty jingle.

The rat buys time 'till after five
Allowing an hour with the wife
Time a plenty to conjure up the famous Blazes magic.
But sod's law he overlooks
Which gets him double-booked
At the Ormond with Lenehan. Oh isn't that just tragic!

Marian: Halcombe that is, not Bloom.
Wilkie's amateur detective we assume
Is personified here, as lovely secretary, Miss Dunne.
She's awoke us from our slumber
And now Boylan, we've got your number.
Miss Dunne, your work here is done.' Scuse pun.

8 REBEL TALES FROM THE CRYPT

An unsteady path briefly lit.
A flickering vesta falls and dies.
Within, conspiratorial shadows
Entomb two men, dark of mien
And hunched in talk.

The priest, eager, strains to learn
Of rebellious times, gone by.
Of Silken and other Geraldines.
Hatchers of plots and witnessed,
Always, by the crypt.

Shaft of light heralds a third
Carried aloft Acolian current
And buffeted by life's head-wind.
Failed with Miles, now tries Ned.
P'raps wind of change?

Must again accept word for deed.
Or here, a sneeze. From Ohio Miles
To Corkish Ned; wind constant.
Long walk for a short drink.
Poor old JJ.

9 BALLS-A-WOBBLIN', EYE-BALLS OGLIN'

Beyond three faces that we recognize
A fresh viz passes before our eyes.
His two events in our story
Serve as his valedictory.
It's Tom Rochford esquire.

Of both events Bloom would approve.
The first, concerns balls in a groove.
Rochford has invented a machine
To identify the particular scene
In the vaudeville theatre.

The other, nothing short of heroism.
For to rescue a man fallen into a chasm
'Neath a manhole where sewery constriction
Heralds his premature extinction,
Deserves no less soubriquet

Stephen's blessing is not as assured.
Writing by machine is not literature
And we recall Stephen Hero's Protean line:
I'd want his life to be his; mine to be mine.
But time yet for interplay.

Lenehan bored; so with McCoy does stroll,
Spots Bloom which prompts his yarn so droll.
Of Molly ogling, of flesh groping.
Of stars perceiving, of Bloom deceiving.
He laughed, he japed.

But the tail of the tale has a sting.
Audience McCoy is not laughing.
Ribald Lenehan has misread the room
Which derives no pleasure from ribbing Bloom.
Mourning favour repaid?

10 YESHU BEN PANTERA

Panther! Panther! Slinking, black
Covert browser. Thumbs to select
Amid savannah of grubby hardbacks
A book for her. To resurrect.

In Eccles den, Tygress preens and sleeks.
Infidelity hour ticks the clock.
Yet still something for her he seeks.
She wanted another by Paul de Kock.

He'll be cuckolded; a racing certainty.
There's Raoul chomping at starter's gate.
Panther exiled; barred without a key
Yet with masochistic thrill, he facilitates.

Pantheras act out Sweets of Sin for real.
In perverse non-fiction rite of passage.
Point of no return and one which we feel,
Will likely make or break their marriage.

But if Pantera and ex-Virgin, Mary-on
Re-engage, renew and resurrect
What would be the state of that union?
Would Stephen give the Presidential Address?

For the last time that this did occur
So goes blasphemous allegoric allegation,
Joseph's Mary slept with centurion Panther
To produce the Saviour of the nation.

11   IT'S CURTAINS

Who will buy these barely used curtains?
Two guineas when new.
No advance Mister, on bid five shillings?
Laquey; clang your gong.
Barang!!

Who can help this family of Simon's?
Was once well to do.
Now Father has only pennies for Dilly.
Laquey; go ding-dong.
Barang!!

Mother dead and father absented.
Sister Monika's soup
May delay a family drowning. But…
Going, going, gone.
Glug, glug.

.

12   KNIGHT OF THE ROAD

Opened are the double doors of the horizon
Unlocked are their bolts.
Kiss of fresh air to bless tea salesman Kernan
Moisten desiccated vaults.

Tea-selling heavy-drinking tongue-biting Tom
Knows his do's; knows his don'ts
Frock-coated, mummified, Empire-champi-on.
Knight of the Road. West British savant.

To customers and back, streets and lanes bestrode.
Well turned out. His mien – majestic.
We hear his stogged thoughts as he pounds the roads.
He's no Socrates but it's peripatetic.

Dollard's masterly rendition of Croppy Boy: trenchant.
Down there, Emmet's last words.
But these radical Fenians seeking Irish independence,
Well, nothing short of absurd.

Poor ol' Tom. Entombed in pyramid of past generation
O'Connell bridge forever Carlisle.
Awake Tom! Break through those doors to a new nation.
Smell that coffee by the Liffey Nile.

13   THE LABYRINTH

A chap built a maze on the island of Crete
So complex, escape was impossible feat.
But with he and son within, this was, well, bittersweet.
But our clever artificer would not accept defeat.

He invented waxen wings so he and the boy might fly.
A run, a jump and up! Need not go terribly high
Just sufficient to clear gorse and wave Minotaur good-bye.
And escape; settle elsewhere. Go forth, multiply.

We know the artificer by the name Daedalus
And we remember that he named his son, Icarus.
If from same lesson we recall, then clever us!
That the ersatz wings were a tad…. ambitious.

Self-compelled to strive, Icarus flew too near the sun.
As melted the wings, down plummeted the son.
Azure Aegean sea! To dive in looks such fun.
But crash from that height and life woebegone.

Likewise, our book features Dedalus and heir;
Simon and Stephen. We may say Dedalii, if we cared.
Jim says this chapter is the labyrinth that ensnares.
So dear reader, these tales we'll compare.

Which segues nicely into the thirteenth vignette.
Stephen browsing; homeless, usurped, depressed.
Paris last winter; thought he'd escaped Irish nets.
But wings clipped, this Icarus reeled back, north-west.

Into lapidary stone, colour of Aegean dark wine
He stares; retrospective arrangement, to ancient time?
Parisian paradise lost. New Eden? Also he can't find..
Creative free-fall. Lassoed by parochial ties that bind.

Across browsed books each costing twopence,
Comes familiar voice of familial presence
His sister Dilly has with Icarian imprudence
Bought French primer, not calorific sustenance.

She looks like Stephen and chips off the old block.
Should have bought food but hit wandering rock.
Will Stephen help cause by returning to the flock?
Would entail self-sacrifice and well, that's not his stock.

Family ship listing badly, he inwardly observes.
Those reporting on deck will be dragged 'neath the surf,
So though agenbite of inwit stabs at his nerve
He selfishly rebuffs; striving for higher cause to serve.

14   HOLD THAT FELLOW

Hold that fellow with the bad trousers;
Hold him now, Ben retorts.
Si Ben Bob in familiar banter,
Joshing and shoving in school yard sport.

Not so for Bloom and all outsiders,
Not for them, easy rapport.
Words rehearsed before being uttered
Still trip over gums instead of doing as ought.

But these bon viveurs of saloon bar and byway,
These are opinionated, self-entitled men.
They josh as they shove as claim they
The city lanes. Big on ego, short on rent.

Amid creditors snarling, Bob seeks time to pay.
Now don't you fret, assuages street lawyer Ben:
Iscariot's pickled, as landlord's levied distrain!
Meaning, nice Reverend Love has the prior intent.

Welcome relief and much thanks to Christian Lord.
But Bob would still like the sub-Sheriff's assur-ence
That scabbard shall restrain the bailiff sword;
That at home an Irishman shall not be harassed

And with such prudent call who would not accord?
A second opinion, yes, because Ben, and no offence,
You yourself are an itinerant of no fixed abode,
Among Dublin's most financially embarrassed.

15   LONG JOHN'S CASTLE

I'm the king of the castle
And you're the dirty rascal.

These are men.
Like Si, like Bob, like Ben
But unlike folk like them,
These men are proper men.

Get things done.
Holed up in Castle Dub.
They make the City run.
Bureaucratic administray-shun.

No layabouts these.
No Iveigh House lodgers these
Wealthy? No, by no means.
But men with responsibilities.

These men matter.
While Si, Ben and Bob natter
Engage in backslapping banter
These work through agenda.

Meeting quor'te.
Council minutes they must report.
Enforce judgements of the court
Official business of various sorts.

Meeting adjourns.
To the wine rooms they sojourn
Of Paddy's death to they learn.
Shall try to do Dignams a good turn.

16   DAMN BAD CAKES

Pat-a cake, Pat-a-cake, Baker man
Bake me a cake as fast as you can.
Not Patrick you eejit but mark it with B
And another for Haines and two cups of tea.

See there in the corner; no cake on his plate
Idée fixe on chessboard; white bishop translates
Not little Jack Horner but our City Marsh-ell
Brother to the brother, it's John Howard Parnell.

Haines takes an interest but that's no surprise.
Authentic Irish sends him misty-eyed.
F'rinstance, page turning the book he just bought
Salivating over Love Songs of Connacht.

He enquires after Stephen, who no-show'd at The Ship
Buck says his mind's gone; prob' lost down the kips.
Or due to lin'g'rin'horror that scared his b'jeezus
As incanted by those zealous chaps of Ignatius.

Haines loves 'em all provided they bearing the green
And he won't be imposed on; must be real Irish cream
To go with his mélange and ooze into his tea.
So goes the afternoon down the DBC.

17 TOOTH OF A RAT

Cashel Boyle O'Connor Fitzmaurice Tisdall Farrell
Names: he has enough of them.
With gaze rapt
And the tooth of a rat,
He wears a very small hat.

Mr.F, is always walking but never in parallel.
Shall be inscribed as his epitaph.
Doing his utmost
To keep those lampposts
How should one say?...innermost.

Zig-zag south-eastward 'long Merrion Square.
Halts; volte-face, gaze still rapt.
Now zig-zags north-west
By Wilde house with Cashel zest
Until visage of preacher Elijah arrests.

Resumes with Justinian protest. Cross him of you dare.
Blindman cometh.. White stick tap-tapping.
Stickumbrella weapon readied
Piranha teeth; to ramming speed.
None so blind as rats who see. Indeed.

18   HIS BOOTS

A man dies.
Big man or little man in stature or girth.
To his son, he's a giant. Someone of worth.

His boots.
To be soled only, for the heals are still good.
Will take some filling but the son feels he should.

New cap.
Black suit too. New to death; no more than a child.
Suddenness of adulthood; neither realized nor reconciled.

Stud collar.
Over-starched, misbehaving, it continues to rise.
To salute the father, up there in the skies.

Comes death
Too soon. Even a city so hardened
Sheds a tear. Its heart is darkened.

From Paddy.
To Patrick. Too soon passes the baton.
So repeats the familiar Dublin pattern.

19   DUDLEY WE HARDLY KNEW YE

The carriages passed by; one then two
Hurroo! Hurroo!
From Phoenix Park by Ormond Quay
They blew, they blew!
Willy the Humble rides with his Lady Miss
Metaphorical backsides for the plebs to kiss
As of our imperial rulers we catch but a glimpse
But Dudley we hardly knew ye.

Obsequious policemen with hats removed,
Salute, salute.
Steely-rims grinding, clattering hooves
Sparks flew, in blue.
Simple Simon bows low but Kernan he stutters
In straining to reach a buttock to pucker,
As the cavalcade parades our betters
But Dudley we hardly knew ye.

At Viceyoy's right hand sits Lady Dudley
Hurroo! Hurroo!
Then Mrs.Paget and Miss de Courcey
But who's that, in blue?
It's Boylan who flashes wink and toothy grill
Gerty strains; do they wear eau de Nil?
As river Poddle its sewage does spill,
But Dudley we hardly knew ye.

Like Conmee, the Viceroy exudes virtue,
It's true, so true.
Drummers and pipers beat the route
Tattoo! Tattoo!
Will hospital charity fare any better
Than Dignam child of Conmee's letter?
Is a mystery Joyce doesn't surrender
And Dudley we hardly knew ye.

Two cheers for Empire's second city
Hurroo! Hurroo!
Sixteenth June goes down in history
It's true, so true.
Not for the cavalcade but a date with Nora
Thence to elope to be Signore and Signora
But through Ulysses the city endur-es!
Yes! Dublin we got to know ye.

ABOUT THE AUTHOR

Russell Raphael was born in Ilford in 1959, the eldest child of Sam a market trader and Valerie a social worker. Like Ilford, unsure of its identity as Essex or east London, Russell has enjoyed his career as a lawyer whilst feeling an Icarus-like urge to strive for deeper creativity and in parallel to his day-job stumbled upon a portal of discovery in James Joyce. Russell is the founder of North London Ulysses a reading group that meets weekly in the pub and online. The Fine Trousers of Almidano Artifoni is a follow up book to his lecture series An Understanding of Ulysses available on kindle from Amazon or in paperback from www.russellraphael.com.

Russell lives in East Finchley, north London with his wife Claire who shares him with West Ham United and their four grown up children.

North London Ulysses. A coming together for all things Ulysses centred around weekly readings in the Muswell Hill/East Finchley corner of north London.

For those further afield there are also weekly online meetings.

www.russellraphael.com

Printed in Great Britain
by Amazon